Café Writers

A First Collection

Published by CAFÉ WRITERS
in Sligo, Ireland, 2014

COPYRIGHT © Café Writers

Printed and bound in Sligo
by Print 2000, Sligo, Ireland

ISBN 978-0-9928490-0-9

Publication of this work is
made possible in part by a
grant from Sligo VEC in 2011

Book design by James Tuomey

Cover image: *The Writing Table*,
photograph by Café group.

The moral rights of the authors
have been asserted

Table of Contents

Foreword by Peggie Gallagher 6

AUTHORS

Maura Gilligan .... 8—25	Emma Purcell .... 80—95
Liam Maloney .... 26—35	Stephanie Ripon .... 96—103
Ann McKirdy .... 36—43	Nora Ryan .... 104—113
Síle Ni Chuirc .... 44—55	Jean Tuomey .... 114—124
Éamon Ó Cléirigh .... 56—65	Biographies 125
Andrew O'Reilly .... 66—79	Table of Illustrations 128

World become Word

Seamus Heaney
The Government of the Tongue
London. Faber & Faber, 1988, 8.

Acknowledgements

We, the Café Writers, are sincerely grateful to the following:

Peggie Gallagher, poet and winner of the Listowel Poetry Collection Award, 2012, for her guidance, editing and encouragement in the production of this first collection from the Café Writers.

The Staff of St. Michael's Family Life Centre for their warmth, welcome and hospitality to all those who visit, work and create within its walls.

Sligo VEC for their encouragement of writing in the community, through a grant in 2011 which has part-funded the publication of this book.

James Tuomey, a talented graphic designer, for his generosity in designing this first collection for us.

Foreword

It was a joy to have been involved with The Cafe Writers in putting this anthology together.

Their open-minded co-operation and energy is what allowed us to hold each individual piece of writing up to the light; always a sobering experience. Through a number of workshops we questioned sentences, sounded out words, weeded adjectives, moved stanzas and paragraphs, trimmed and cut back.

Different voices remind us that language can capture very different kinds of experience. Each poem, short story and extract is self-contained, a unique source we can return to in moments of remembrance.

The Cafe Writers have already won national and international acclaim from the many literary prizes they have received and their numerous publications.

With gratitude to all of the writers for allowing me to participate in this diverse and exciting collection. I wish this talented group every success with their future publications.

Peggie Gallagher

Café
Writers

Maura Gilligan

Image: Detail from *To a Child Dancing in the Wind*
Watercolour on paper by Maura Gilligan

Requiem

If an orchestra had played
there would have been
a dominance of cello;
low mournful notes
suspended,
trembling.

but there was no
orchestra,
just the call
of seals
at Oyster Lane
and the moaning
of wind
around Knocknarea.

A morphine pump clicked,
delivered fleeting oblivion.
The scent of neroli
hung in the air.
In the room where
our dreams began
we were alone again
when you left

to wage war
upon the stars.

Maura Gilligan

Diamonds in the Flat Field

In soft green
aftergrass

each blade
supports

its own new
dewdrop

freshly fallen
at the dawn

to balance
here awhile

before submitting to
the sun's evaporation

the boot's obliteration
the wind's swift transportation

or drowning
in the rain.

The transient
moment sparkles.

Close to Classiebawn

Blue wisp-streaked heaven.
White mist snakes along
the valley floors.

The harbour at Mullaghmore
lies beyond the bend where
Connemara ponies graze

and early sunlight illuminates
the rounded belly of a
late-foaling mare.

Boats sit at anchor.
Razor-fish strew damp sand.
Oyster-catchers strut

the water's frilly edge
while buried in the sedge
secrets lie –

souvenirs of carnage in
this bay
one hot July.

Maura Gilligan

In the Restless Hours

I hear the cry of a vixen,
she is very near

Her screech awakens neighbouring
dogs, one high on the mountainside

close to where she cries
in undergrowth, another far

below, on the road that skirts the sea.
No stars light her way.

Dampness cloaks Culleenduff,
seals are silent,

the strand below awaits another tide.
In the space between her sirening,

soft sounds of moisture
seep from leaf to earth.

Winter Evening on the Island

Nature's dimmer switch
gradually
turns the light down
on the 3rd of November
and sends
a rosy filter
spilling
like a soft scarf
onto the hills,
the lighthouse,
the ocean,
the cold grass
and the whitewashed walls.
Blues, greens and white
shine
through a pink muslin haze
and sounds walk in
the kitchen door.
The rhythmic chomping of
winter grass
in the mouths of cows
is disturbed
by the spluttering
of a boat
crossing Shrúnamíle.
A curlew calls,
and the loud whisper
of a flock
of starlings
landing
cuts his long note
short.

Maura Gilligan

Out of Arigna

Driving home from Arigna
through rolling hills
that have sprouted windmills
and fat summer hedges

I slow down as I pass
an old man on a Honda,
his collie stretched
across his knees

A metal helmet disguises
his identity,
his Honda weaves through
an invisible chicane,

his dog's tail indicates left.

Reilig

Passing the grey wall
I think of you

and in the bleak blast
of October hail

I see the earth
for the first time

as your blanket,
and I am glad

that you will no longer know
days of darkness

and bitter skies.

Maura Gilligan

Inismulclohy

... a lullaby

Seaweed, crackling dried and spurned
seabirds where the current churns
oyster catchers, gulls and terns

.... evening on the Island

Moonlight, silver on the strand
Oyster Island's light commands
a gentle, brief attention span

.... night time on the Island

Knocknarea in stillness sitting
dewdrop grass makes wet feet glisten
shellfish spitting if you listen

.... morning on the Island.

*[Inismulclohy is an ancient name for
Coney Island in Sligo Bay]*

Seals at Oyster Lane

At the verge of the road beneath the southern face of Knocknarea, Oyster Lane drops steeply seaward, narrow and deeply rutted. Briars stretch in vicious embrace before the laneway opens suddenly to the west where the channel flows, touching the round brown stones of the shore.

Beyond that channel sealbanks sprawl across the bay to Beltra, sandy islands supporting colonies of black, white and beige sea mammals. Seal pups sit and wobble and watch. Young seals dive and play and bite shining sea-trout, ending the momentum of their journey into Ballisodare Bay. Older seals sit stately as the incoming tide rises about them, and their heads gradually disappear. Seeming never to have moved, they re-appear as the water recedes, as if to take a curtain call.

The seals make constant stolen sounds – like humans, they mutter and moan, like wild geese they honk, like dogs they bark and growl, like wolves they howl. Most eerily of all they wail, conjuring the cry of the banshee in a lament that rises and spreads and soars. The sheer cliffs of the mountain at Culleenamore hold the long notes of their wailing, and in rocky crevices the sleep of ravens is disturbed.

Humble Escort

A tiny seahorse in a tomb of clear plastic and delicate shells once sat on the dashboard of my old Ford Escort. Below the little sea-scene, an old silver St. Christopher icon shone. I removed the sea ornament, but kept St. Christopher. The church had demoted him from the post of Protector of Travellers in recent times, but I chose to believe in his power to protect my little passengers. It was the eighties and we had bought the car from a friend of ours for two hundred pounds. I thought it was wonderful. My freedom-to-go machine.

I can still feel the sun's heat and the prickle of sand on my feet as I drive home barefoot from the beach with the kids in the navy Escort, all the windows down, a breeze rippling in to fan our faces. We are returning from our favourite place, a tiny cove hidden in a corner of the great sweeping arc of Culleenamore Beach. Known as the Sandy Field, this small scimitar of sand, shingle and stone curves below small cliffs of compressed oyster shells – the kitchen midden of ancient ancestors. The tide fills the nearby channel, spilling into the small cove to create its shallow bathing pool. Hollows in the grass above hold all the paraphernalia of a summer picnic. The sheer western cliff of Knocknarea rises above us and the Ox Mountains sit across the water from us. Sometimes the cliffs above us catch the childrens' voices, returning an echo that floats above the channel.

Unbidden, another Culleenamore memory returns. Willie had driven the Escort there to go fishing. He had left me the "good" car for the day. Strangely, I can't recall what the "good" car was at that time, but I can see the old navy Escort parked on the prickly grass by the shoreline as darkness fell. The fisherman hadn't returned, and I had gone to look out for him. Should I should walk out the two mile stretch of the bay to the fishing shelf at Banc Bán? My eyes adjusting to the filtered twilight allowed me a glimpse of a silhouette in the shadow of the far-off dunes. The image solidified as I concentrated. I recognised his walk, fishing rod on one shoulder and the two moving dots that were the spaniels at his heels. My relief dissolved, annoyance surfaced. His adventuring often triggered my fears of darkness, of murky hunting wetlands, of the dark side of the tide at Polcurraigh at this moment, of it's soft steep sand banks and its power to steal even those who knew its ways well.

At home, putting lamps and hot water on, I watched late summer twilight shift from rose to gold to a blue night sky that held stars out over the bay. The familiar roar of the old Escort's engine flying up our steep driveway shattered the peace as the kettle sang at cocoa-time.

If it was a successful night the salt-encrusted canvas satchel would spill a sea-trout or two or three onto the sink where sand and silver scales and sea-lice clung to the steel before being swirled away on their final watercourse.

1966, CALCUTTA

My father drives us home from the Club.

He has given Marcandai the night off. We love the times he drives us himself. Sweat beads keep gathering on his brow and his large white handkerchief is damp. The streets are quiet now. Above the door of the Moulin Rouge Restaurant pink electric blades turn slowly.

Further down the street the lights of the Blue Fox blink in a bright square around their blue neon symbol. Dad indicates right at the entrance to Stephen Court. Driving through the short concrete tunnel a wave of longing for the open road assails me and I imagine us, crossing the River between the high iron arms of Howrah Bridge, all the car windows open, creating the breeze the hot night denies us.

The tunnel we drive through gives onto the rutted road that leads to the apartments, passing by the servants' quarters on either side. Through the archway Stephen Court stands stout and sprawling, a low colonial building tucked behind Park Street. Its apartments are large and old, with a long cement verandah fronting each one. No. 3 is on the first of three floors, and the palm trees flanking the entrance have grown to its verandah level.

The lift shimmies to a halt, leaving a narrow dark slit where it doesn't quite touch the landing. The liftman calls goodnight and clangs the heavy gate shut. The old machine wheezes and grunts and descends slowly. It's just two paces to the cream double doors of the apartment. The black mouth of the concrete stairwell mocks. The right half of the door gives in to the turn of the key, and a shiver snakes down my damp back. The stairwell is a dark cavern that frightens me. On the ground floor, the liftman's wooden sandals clack across worn marble, connected to his soles by a single knob that his toes clutch.

It amazes us that the liftman's toes can cling to the single stud between the big toe and the second toe, propelling him forward on wooden platforms. His pallet and blanket await him in the wide bare hallway open to the night.

The hot Calcutta night hums.

A dry rustle in the palms whispers a hoarse invitation to sleep on the verandah, and we plead with our parents to let us camp there. The verandah overlooks the yard at the back of the YMCA building where we see Muslims facing Mecca and praying on small coloured mats each morning and evening. The convex top of the verandah is broad enough to lean across without ever touching the edge, its coat of cream gloss paint is cracked into jigsaw patterns under the assault of the sun.

I watch the stars, think of Divali, the Festival of Light, when hundreds of tiny tea lights line the balconies and verandahs of the servants' quarters behind our bedroom. Each year I peer into the long low building through the wire window grid, never tiring of watching the flickering lights.

My forehead carries the mark of the grid... tiny squares of dust are etched onto my brow.

When I am tall enough to see myself in the spotted mirror over the basin, I wonder at the design. Years later, Lenten ashes on the brows of pedestrians on wet Irish Ash Wednesdays would recall my childhood insignia.

In the white hot daytime fat black and yellow Ambassador taxi cabs swarm through thronged streets.

Every second vehicle blows its horn incessantly – a mad a'capella choir down Park Street and along the broad boulevard of Chowringhee. Chowringhee holds the first skyscraper I have ever seen. In retrospect this building may have been a high rise block, but as a child the word 'skyscraper' held me in thrall.

A gigantic billboard on that building holds the words 'She loves you YEAH, YEAH, YEAH' plastered below the smiling dark-suited images of the Beatles. Incongruous above the teeming millions of Calcutta's streets and the traffic lights where the blinded beggar stands.

Mr. Jordan, my father's Armenian friend with the glistening gold front tooth tells us that the beggar boy was maimed by his parents as a baby to garner sympathy and a few coins from the incessant stream of cars.

I always dread the moment the car crawls to a stop at those lights.

On the back seat with my siblings, windows wide open in the glaring heat, I see the figure of the beggar come nearer in his halting walk from car to car. Grey rags on his thin body and grey opaque pools where his eyes should have shone. In another flashback many years later something of the menace of those moments returns in the approach of charity collectors at traffic lights. The beggars of Calcutta had mined this lode decades ago.

I remember gold glistening all about us in the middle of the covered market as my first watch is bought at the jeweller Tejoohmal's, I see white cotton saris hitched to avoid open drains between the stalls, brown-eyed babies travelling on their mothers' hips, the babble of shoppers and traders softened by the clinking of silver, gold and glass bangles on brown wrists and the gentle jingling of ankle bells, the scent of jasmine blossoms adorning sleeked-back hair, talk of strikes and another Hindu-Muslim riot, skimpy shelters of the people who live and cook on the streets, red spittle produced by the chewing of the pan leaf on the pavements, the dusty footpaths and walls where those without even a skimpy shelter slept... I recall the diamond in Indira Desai's nose catching the light as she performed her Indian dance for us, our school's preparations for the arrival of the Queen, our short white P.E. dresses, standing for hours in the Governor's Palace in polite rows, the bright light outside creating silhouettes as the dignitaries finally approach, Prince Philip's smile which seemed to beam straight at me.

I hear the noise of a stone grinding spices reverberating through our apartment, hear the train to Ranchi chugging northwards through unfamiliar rocky green territory on its two-day journey, feel the crush of bodies at each station we stop at, wonder at little villages that seem to grow out of the red earth.

Maura Gilligan

Images of Saturday morning breakfasts at the swimming club with Dad, blue water and ground that burned our bare feet, monkeys screeching in the trees bordering the army barracks, papayas on the glass-topped table for breakfast, blisters on my brother's back from the sun, breeze from a ceiling fan, my mother's hands easing a stomach ache, small lizards making their way to the cool green wall near the verandah ceiling, and going home on leave, looking forward to feeling the beautiful cold when the door of the plane opens at Dublin Airport – the novelty of wearing a jumper.

Liam Maloney

Image: *Hands*,
Photograph by Liam Maloney

Beautiful people

Beautiful people never wait in queues
get blisters from ill-fitting shoes
or bleed from paper cuts.

Beautiful people never have to hide
inside the forgotten attic box
of a submarine meant to sail the skies.

Liam Maloney

Caffeine cartography

He ran after her.
She, the leaver of a scarf
behind, quietly, on a table. In
the rush, an exchange of absent complexities,
a mug rattled. The coffee splash
formed a shimmering image of
Aztec Mexico before
the Spanish came.

Hillside art

Woman, 53, panting
wears a blue plastic bag
carries a chequered tweed knee-length coat
last in style, summer 1994
scales the hill at Connaughton Road car park, Sligo
it's only a little hill –
but still.

Where has she been seen before? Was it
in a Swedish pornographic film?
Directed by a Marlboro chain smoker called Benny Bergstrom,
who favoured black and white cinematography
over large breasts.

Woman, 53, panting
it's only a little hill –
but still.

Liam Maloney

July metronome

He tells
his heart
there is
no other
just her.

She is
the sweet
July breeze
that pours
through
every tree.

One branch
shivers
and drops
a prize.

She is
this leaf
that he
will press
between
the pages
of his book.

Listen closely

Eavesdropper, once punished by Anglo-Saxon law,
stealing thigh bones from other's conversations.

A beautiful woman, who got married in Utah,
is overheard as she speaks into a mobile phone
her Briel Milano watch sparkles in the apparent drudgery.

She says: 'Goodbye, I love you.'

There are always places to listen,
somewhere between the long grass
and the setting sun.

Memory foam

Each return is the same:
Did we ever leave this carnival of angst?

Handshake still firm for these are farmer's hands
eyes have changed colour, a 3% reduction
in visionary understanding since the last trip.

A south-west wind caresses, rumbles
so we stand, holding unspoken words,
at the corner of Foley's field,
gathering dust.

Olive eater

He still eats olives from dampened cardboard caskets
the pitted ones, green, soaked in brine
each morsel a preserved reminder of a former lover.

She was so formal then: Lights had to be switched off,
her Facebook page checked first
before the strands of pity were unravelled
thighs prised apart just to keep his moods intact.

He would like to recall that he ate olives from her scented belly button
or that secret place where her Venus halos met
as she tapped her lacquered nails on the kitchen countertop,
looking at the ceiling, dripping indifference.

Liam Maloney

Shooting star

A man, 63, shoots himself,
eyeshadow unhappiness.

In his dirty kitchen, bags of burnt toast
suggested an exact disposition.

Faceless Jacob will die of thirst
his ship, forever stalled, on a frozen sea.

Ann McKirdy

Image: *The View from our Kitchen*
Acrylic on paper by Sarra McKirdy

We Lived by Numbers

The measures of childhood
on the western seaboard
facing Belmullet's Atlantic,
the sea one ditch away
across O'Malley's field.

Our neighbour Michael Kavanagh
manned the weather station,
where we were never allowed to go.
We'd hear it on the news;
'Malin Head to Mizen Head
Carnsore Point to Valencia'
the next line in the song was ours,
'Belmullet, 10 knots, rising slowly.'

We knew numbers,
everyone's telephone number;
ours, Belmullet, 68
Granny's, Balla, 173
our friends, in the North, Aughnacloy, 267.

Daddy was a numbers' man,
read the ashes paper,
wore red elastic bands on his wrist;
but he couldn't remember a shoe size.
He measured our feet with string.

The Key of B

Stand close to the roaring stones
as the last breaking wave crashes ashore
pounding stones

Filtering harmony
becoming beach music

Listen
as the backwash
rakes and stirs

Listen
to the awakening,
the percussion rhythm and then
silence.

Listen
as it creeps away
a shy musician
fading into the vast ocean.

Through Time

We had our faces pressed
to the same pane of glass
looking out
at 'our landscape'
if an observer can possess anything.

We let it fill us, Dad
not knowing the other's
soul would dance
through briars and reeds
of another time.

Your snipe
your pheasant
your bog
companions to me
winged Souls.

Death's Beauty

I stood on a mountain
thinking of you
in October –
the thief of colour
warmth and light
had stolen you away.

I remember the nest of you,
laid out
on white sateen
where you always used to sit.

The inane commentary on death's beauty;
'doesn't he look lovely?'
A knife through my chest.

When the billows of life
blew through you
they were blind.

'Don't heed them, put your head down and say nothing'
would be your advice;
but you're not here.
Just the lonesome nest of you.
You have flown away.

A Day Of Lessons

Saving lupin seeds in November
drying them
a note to plant their tap roots in another two weeks.
And lilies of the valley
grow from bulbs that spread northwards.

Picasso has much in common with Joyce,
his imagery
translated onto canvas
Joyce's demons on to paper.

We are not supposed to talk about madness or endings.
Yet it is in this darkness,
the seed is nurtured, the artist created,
and the human being
if lucky,
will emerge

like the caterpillar
from an envelope of darkness
to open its wings.

Ann McKirdy

Síle Ní Chuirc

Image: *Istanbul Street*
Acrylic on paper by Síle Ní Chuirc

Grandparents

One day, a long time after my mother's death, while clearing out a box of knick knacks that had been in her house, an old photo fell out of a book. It was of a man and woman obviously taken on their wedding day sometime in late 1800. It was examined to see if there was some family resemblance. They are both standing at a small table. She is dressed in a cream lace teagown with a high ruffed neck, her hair dark and glossy in a high bouffant, she gazes with a soft shy half smile out at the camera. He stands slightly behind her, very straight and severe with an intense look in his eyes. This is not a man to be trifled with. One hand rests on the table and the other on his hip. He wears a three piece suit with high collar and white bow tie. There is a gold fob chain with a medal hanging from it lying across his waistcoat. This is clue number one. Another clue is to be seen in the corner of the photo. It is the name of the photographer. It says, 'Stanley, Dublin.' The mystery deepens.

Time passes, I make a copy of the photo and give it around to my family. Everyone oohs and aahs over it and wonders and wonders. We like the mystery, we don't really want to delve too deeply. It's nice to speculate. Then one day an historian friend sees it and says, 'I think I know what that medal stands for'. He goes offf and googles and comes back and says with great gravitas 'That is a campaign medal from the Afghan war! This man served in an eight year campaign in India. He was under the command of Earl Frederick Sleigh Roberts of Kandahar'. In 1880 he was on the long march from Kabul to relieve Kandahar which was being attacked by the Afghans. This medal was given for distinction of service. These are my Grandparents!

The Afghan campaign ended in 1888. As my grandmother came from Co. Kildare this wedding probably took place in the Curragh Military Camp, when he came home from India.

Now I remember, when my mother talked about her father, she said that he was addressed as 'Sir' by his children, that he had a portrait of Earl Frederick Sleigh Roberts hanging on the landing of the house, and every night when he climbed the stairs to bed he stopped before the portrait and saluted his commanding general. Having read more about the famous general I understand that he was beloved by his troops, having fought in the Boer war and receiving the Victoria Cross. He was known as 'Bobs' by his men. I remember too that my mother said her father would stand and look at the night sky and tell his children the names of all the stars in our galaxy. He must have used the night sky as a compass when on the long night marches through the mountains and passes of Afghanistan. I like to imagine that I have inherited some of his love of open spaces and far off places. When I look at the night sky I always think of him.

In Fear of Becoming Beige

Fading into the background was not for Daisy. Her walls were decorated with flowers cut from magazines. Because she didn't have a garden her kitchen became a blooming paradise. As the mood struck, her shoes were painted at the same time as the room. She was the first woman to have mint green shoes to match her hat.

She had spent her youth in America, and her speech was peppered with little gems, such as 'on the sidewalk' and pulling the 'drapes'. This imbued her with glamour when she eventually came home to her little town. People loved her hats. When asked where they came from, she replied with great aplomb, 'why Wannamakers of Fifth Avenue, of course'. It didn't matter that they had been second hand from rich ladies wardrobes. She added brooches and pearl drops, to add to the effect.

At seventeen she had fallen in love with a young man, whom she said was the spitting image of Robert Taylor. It didn't matter that he didn't come up to scratch. She loved beautiful things, and he filled the bill. In a photograph taken in Central Park in New York, he leans against the railings of a bridge, dressed in a beautiful suit, gazing into the camera with languorous grace.

But the beautiful man hated America, and with every fibre of his being he yearned for home. He looked for it in crowded bars, in busy streets, in undergrounds. It was a hole in his heart that only home could fill. So they set sail for Queenstown.

It took seven days to cross the Atlantic. But when they reached their destination, life was no happier. Marcel Proust said that, 'the compulsion to travel, the restlessness that means you can't sit still, is a fundamental flaw'. So we spend all our lives searching.

He departed this life not long after, and she was left a young widow. Did she fade into obscurity? Not a bit of it. She carried on in her flamboyant way. Her youthful adventures became fantasies that kept her friends in thrall. In old age her mantra was 'I haven't laid eyes on a handsome man for forty years'.

Untitled

Into a field of bones at the end of a dirt track
Where the grasses stir gently
Seductive whisperings
'Come close come closer smell the nectar
Come push the door and enter.'
It is high summer
Before the turning of the leaf
The youth sighs
His first glimpse of Eden takes his breath away.

The Adventures of Sam and Pip

One split egg, and there they were, little mirror images of one another, warm in a cave, DNA and brain cells shared. I knew them for a long time, but they were intimate with one another for just as long. When little minnow eyes popped out, 'ho ho, little bro, pleased to meet ya, and glad you're another man child.' Months and months went by, both fighting for space and eyeballing each other, because of course, they didn't know anything about time, they didn't know me. Time was in the future, and so was I. They didn't know that when all the fingers and toes and wobbly bits were finally there, that was when the big adventure would begin.

In the meantime; when one turned around there was that pesky kid still there, a heel stuck under a nose, a finger tickling a rib. Less and less room to move, those things that grew on the side of the face, now they were interesting. Little bro would jump and fidget after those things grew. That tasted nice too, that thing that grew in a bunch. Other little man child liked the taste of that. Eventually they stopped fighting for space, they came to some arrangement; one lay at the back of the cave propped on his elbow, sucking the smaller of the bunch of things, while the thing that grew on the side of his face felt a boom de boom and a gurgling. The other sat upright at the front with the thing that grew on the side of his face pressed against the wall. Ho, ho, that was weird. He felt like tapping his feet to that tum de tum and da de da da.

Well now, it was quite pleasant that territorial rights were established. It was warm and if bro number two, at the front position, felt like communicating, he just gave a great heave and turned around. This seemed to cause consternation beyond the wall, a sound joined the tum de tum and became 'oooagh.' All was quiet and peaceful for a time, and they grew fat and happy in their little cavern. Suddenly, one day, all the warm stuff surrounding them went whoosh!. Bro number two flipped on his head, and nosedived after it. But the tunnel was small and dark, and he had to squeeze his bunches tight by his side. He couldn't turn around because his head was stuck, worse still, he was alone. He decided to wiggle a bit and like a fish he swam towards the entrance.

Meanwhile, back in the cave, Bro number one, startled out of his reverie, watched the rear portion of his brother disappearing. Out popped his thumb, and off he went in pursuit. It was tough going, but he was determined to find out what was at the end of the tunnel.

Síle Ní Chuirc

To Paul

He wings high upon the seventh set
through caverns of viridian hue.
Above, the murderous surf
sings out its song
of currents, rips, and crooked seas.
Who love me come and catch
my transluscent tube
my thundering beat.

Ride with me
on chariots of ecstasy
through seas of raging foam
that endlessly roll, on and on
to some horizon new.
Come catch me now
and glide forever on my crest.

On War

Black birds against an angry sky
Flapping burkas in the aftershock
Encircling little ones in their wings
These are the victims of mans' bad dreams
Their eyes show the terror
As they search for bread to feed their young.

Running men arms full of plunder
Golden vases filled with plastic flowers
Computers, fridges, freezers
Bringing home the spoils of war to mud huts
Where mothers wait for bread to feed their young.

Strategies, plans, great armoured divisions
Moving on a coloured map
Through ancient sites of civilization
Bomb craters where hanging gardens once bloomed
Now mothers wait for bread to feed their young.

Where is the manna once that fell from Heaven?
On the plains between two great rivers
That fed the followers of the man of vision
Is it because they call You by a different name
That women wait in vain for food to feed their young?

Síle Ní Chuirc

Éamon Ó Cléirigh

Image: *Lough Gill*
Photograph by Eamon O'Cleirigh

A Thin Shield

She sits by her window,
lace curtain masking reality,
counting her true friends
on the tip of her finger.

The evening sun's dance
on her window sill does nothing
to lighten shadows, dark whispers
of times gone by stretching distance

to a freedom beyond;
colour, sound, the business
of normality – each passerby blind to
her silent pain.

Hindsight's unwanted weight
burdens her tired heart.
Her window remains shut,
a thin shield against inevitability.

Éamon Ó Cléirigh

An Observation On The Day Of A Christening

Crow, on your bough,
cast your knowing eye
through my morning window.
White smoke rising in the valley
merges with the hungry cries
of babies with no choice.
Will sacred oils ease the pain
of life, or has the crow's
shadow already decided where
Sligo's early mist will
carry your message to the world?

Curtain Call

Rain slides across Maedhbh's
hilltop tomb, like curtains
closing on a final act.

Gulls rise from the Garavogue
in applause, screaming
for an encore.

Light splits the cloud,
stretching shadows as far
as the rainbow's edge.

Life's auditorium must
be cleared and cleaned in
time for the next show.

Éamon Ó Cléirigh

Good Faith

She placed a teaspoon
in a bright red envelope
and dropped it into
her local river,
hoping that hope itself
would activate, and
happiness would come
her way.

She'd heard about it
from a friend,
who had it on good faith
that it couldn't fail.

She pauses everyday
on her way to town,
willing her hope pack
to shift from its watery perch,
trapped behind a rock.

Morning Tea at Rosses Point

Winter folds beneath glazed impressions
of spring. A mountain stream, fingers spread,
chases an ebbing tide leaving
with the knowledge of a world in waiting.

I touch fossils of thought
before turning to a waking sun,
the balance of my day reflected
in lengthened shadows of intention.

We drink our tea on a bench
overlooking pain and solitude,
savour the taste of a far horizon,
its curve a slow embrace.

Éamon Ó Cléirigh

Moon Haiku

deep angled shadow
crooked on my stairway
a full moon canvas

One Instance

Rain brings the need to ground,
to find a common base, a shelter
for loose ends. Ancient roots
cross my path, directing, guiding,
each step resonates and gives
notice of intention.

Errant voices chase serenity, while
heavy-laden fear of truth blocks
our bridge to inspiration. If only I
could move to the other side of the
oak, disappear, dwell in silence,
for one breath, one instance of quality.

The rain, my friend, drowns out
the sound of pain.

Éamon Ó Cléirigh

Strandhill Stone

She watches the morning sun slip
around Culleenamore Bay, bringing
light to a settling stone long journeyed
through heartbreak and hope.

Shadows stretch as sands tread
trails across her map of sorrows,
her heart cold to memories in
a searching breeze.

Waves crash, disperse remembered time;
shapes that once defined her day.
They draw the past beneath, dissolve blame,
its rigid harness loosened, future glimpsed.

She places the stone in her bag.
They will no longer suffer
the pain of solitude.

Andrew O'Reilly

Image: *Cafe Arabica, Sligo*
Photograph by Andrew O'Reilly

The Conversation

It was a conversation that had started before I got there, so there was no point of reference for me, I didn't know the people yet the conversation pulled me in. I couldn't tell you why but it had really reeled me in and was continuing to do so, and if either of the people talking had noticed this stranger listening in to their conversation they would have been fully entitled to cry, "D'ya mind not listening," or maybe to look at me and say something in a cutting tone like, "What do you think?".

This of course would have thrown me completely as I'd have had little response because I'd only come in to get some relief from the heat of the day. Something cool to wet my throat. Still, I opted for a coffee and as it worked out the seat I got was probably the last one in the café, and wouldn't you know it was situated right beside the coffee machine. I was in the middle of Paris at the height of the tourist season so maybe they just had not noticed the stranger listening, for it must have been plain to them that that's what I was doing.

I had to wonder though why was I doing this? Was it their body language or maybe their clothes? Everybody talks about the way French people dress. So I stopped and looked at them again, and that's when I realised the people had gone. Where had they gone? More's to the point, when did they go? And who were those two people who were now looking at me as I looked at their table?

Suddenly I felt very flustered around the face and started to make feeble movements around my station, checking my bags, making like I had forgotten something. Asking the barmaid for a glass of water, which I downed in one gulp, then having paid my bill I quickly left through a side entrance. Stopping to see which way to go, I spied the people who had been talking. Had they gone outside because they were irritated by my listening to them, or were they up to no good? I decided not to find out.

Turning a corner, I disappeared up the crowded boulevard amongst all the people in this busy capital, probably the fashion home of the world. With a rich history of seedy jazz clubs, broken dreams and sordid romances, and some of the finest architecture the world has ever seen.

Travels in Colour

Hold that thought then count to three but hush there my love, for sometimes there are no words to describe a moment nor find the way that really conveys how you felt at the time. How I found myself, standing beside you, yet this time we were parting ways, not departing on one of the many journeys we had gone on before today. The strings of my heart were being pushed, pulled and played one way till all the other could do was to go the other. I didn't know whether I was coming or going. But what I did know, was how this felt like nothing ever had before. I had seen so many amazing things on travels with you but all was blurred now from the tears in my eyes. Many a beautiful clear blue daybreak followed by a golden sunset, all I could see was a blackness in front of me.

Andrew O'Reilly

It Just Happened That Way

It had been a really long day and I had gotten very little done, though I'd I mean this was all amongst friends; nobody wished the other any harm, well at least that's what they would have told you had you asked. I mean all we wanted was the best outta life, and in the end what harm could come from it? In fact we all could have made a few quid from the project along with getting our handled pressure like this before and come out on top so this should have been a snap. names in print. As for the art work, well if I could I'd just as soon leave that to somebody else. That really was not my scene.

I'm at the last place, or worst I wish to be at right now, printing this piece out in an internet café, word following word. There is no honour in what I do here, but I knew if something like this was not done, well then there would be nothing to show in the morning. I should feel some sort of shame, knowing as I do this will get an utter bollocking in the morning. Still, I sit here just wishing something would happen; some sort of inspiration. A poem to the forlorn maybe. Yeah, maybe that's what I could say this is to all those out there who try to get a novel out. Something for those who believe that saying "everyone has a story in them".

If the technical end of things had worked out this might have been avoided, but that was just not to be, and now I feel like the runt of the litter, the last one at the bowl. With no food left on offer, there is nothing but these scraps on the page. Why should you wonder why this author will never get a publishing deal?

A Bit of What You Like

Short stories or poems, you know, really it didn't matter. What did matter was what you enjoyed. I mean, if after the curtain went down and you found yourself walking into a cold night after the price of a ticket all you can think of is, I wonder what's on telly – then I'd be pissed. For me there is something creative going on, writing and making up each story and its characters, even of how to describe certain people, that whole giving them a background. What makes them important to the story. Still, even as I write this down I'm reminded of the part that I really get a kick out of, which is the reading. If you asked me to describe how I write it would be that of one who does screenplays. I'm not locked into that whole punctuation thing which some people are. But no matter what I write about from day to day, fact or fiction, poetry or prose, whatever, it's those who surround me who have a lot to do with what comes out on the page.

Funny or curious things may enter my mind, ending up as part of the story in its telling, which may never have entered my mind during the writing stage .And that's fine for I will always make my way back to the place where I wandered. Sam Phillips to Johnny Cash, "Wait, wait, we don't do stuff like that." Johnny says, "Well, what about... do you do anything about..." Well anyhow, that's how the story goes. What I'm saying is it's all about what you do when your back's against the wall. It's then that ability shows itself. I can't say for sure what is the best time or place, but I know where I'm at my ease. But outside of it a laziness creeps in. Or maybe it's just my creative mode sits in the idle position and this saddens me. For the times I do get going and am active again, well, it's not as hard as I always imagine it to be, or maybe there is not a wall in front of me. A wall that's not there, but I feel exists.

Music, Music, Music

Somehow it all made sense. Nobody had ever brought it this close to me before. Now I felt an understanding as to what all the fuss was about. I could see it in their eyes and on the faces as the dancers moved. This was an awakening, a birth of something new to me. My music collection meant more to me, kind of like feeling what those people making music at the start felt. The music I'd been brought up on was, well, you see I was lucky, it was always around me.

My family was always listening to music morning, noon and night. It was hard not to have a love for it. Mum and Dad loved Jazz and had seen many of the great artists. Those who for me, well, I could only imagine what it was like watching Ella Fitzgerald as she sang the Cole Porter songbook. Or maybe Sinatra and Basie jamming together. Still, all that had to change, and so it did, for you see my elder brothers, one two years, the other seven years older than me, brought the music of the day into the house. So my parents had to give some time over to Punk/Ska and a touch of Reggae. In other words the place where I grew up was a melting pot of music.

Still, forgive me as I've been wandering far from where this piece was supposed to be going. It was meant to be about a town, or as they would call it, a county, and it was surrounded by many others, all of them so far removed from the area I had grown up. This place owed me nothing, and for much of my formative times here, well, I had had nothing but bad luck and misfortune. I'll never forget how this place was described to me. I'd never have imagined that you'd still find me here. Never will forget the words my dad said to me, as the three of us walked down the street. He and mom had come up for a long weekend. What he said was, "Never have I seen one person affect those around him."

Don't know that I'd go so far in full agreement, but that's what he said. At this point some words my English teacher said to me come back to me. She said always write about what you know to be true, that's not to say never do fiction but just what's true to you. So having said that, I can tell you that much of what lies within is of my past.

European Flavours

There surely would be much to check out in this little seaside town. Still searching, looking for something that resembles, something that conjures up, that will match past glories, but they seem to be hard to come by. I remember a story once written about a café. I was there on the day. It was a Sunday I believe and there were a lot of people there and it was very noisy. It was a place I liked to go but is no longer in town. Like so many places in this current economic gloom they just seem to have a small life span, but still while it was there it added to this small town. Many of its regular clients would have been there and I was one of them. There was a French Market in town that weekend which added to the festivities. There was also music, a small jazz band. It was one of the reasons it had made itself such a good attraction, one of the hot spots, the food was good and the people who worked there were friendly. The name of the place is, well I'm not going to mention that just yet. Still, it was just off the main thoroughfare in the town.

I had taken my usual seat in the corner. I was able to get the attention of any of the people working there very easily, which suited my needs very well. I don't remember what I ordered, but I can tell you they had some very tasty things on the menu, if they were a little pricey. But it was worth it. I had remembered all the names of the people who worked there through musical association. Well, I had to find an easy way as many of the names were not of an English origin. I found this to work very well, though at this point I'm afraid I cannot remember much about them. I do know much of my time had been spent looking at all those on the street out front. There was a certain joy to watch them, all the different shapes and sizes and the different coloured clothes walking past.

The volume around me suddenly rose to an incredible pitch. I was stuck in a corner seat and didn't have to look far to see why. The band had stopped playing and all those talking in the café were now a force to be reckoned with. To me it was just another diversion and other noises started up: the foods and wines that were being ordered along with all the empties being thrown into a big black bin. This place could have been anywhere! I mean it, there was a vibrancy to it all that did not make me think of home.

Part of what added to this was the people and the mix of ages, and it was obvious from all the different dialects that the diners where of a European flavour. I'm sure it was as much a shock to them as it was to me. I'd not been in town all that long and this was like a clarion call.

Andrew O'Reilly

Easy Does It Now

That may be so, I mean, you tell me they are very user friendly but I never found that to be the case. Everything I gave them, nothing was enough, or good enough I should say. Me now, I'm, well, I like to think of myself as one who doesn't push folks.

Careful prodding, that's the way. Using that method is more likely to gain a result or the result you're after. It's all about how you treat those around you. Getting their attention, and once it's yours, you are on the way to getting. I mean, you have them. Well, then anything is possible if you can maintain that status quo. So go on then, and what holds people more than something happy?

I'm sorry, I just can't do that. Don't get me wrong, it's not that I'm an unhappy person, but I try to maintain a level of the reality around a situation. So the web I'm spinning, whatever that may be, has to be one that could happen to any of those around me. I must have one thing to base it around. One that each of these folk can relate to. Something so amazing it creates characters, inspiring good and evil. Whilst you're doing all this you yourself have created a transformation and found yourself as the playwright, within your very own web, one in which you have been telling these people it's really like an opening night. If you can just picture it – the house is full, the chord is pulled and the first lines are spoken. Whether you get what you're after is like waiting to read the reviews the very next morning.

Questions

Wonder who stays in there? I only ask cos I've never seen anyone enter and well, I've not seen a person leave. It reminds me of a place I stayed in once. Funny place it was, the family stayed for the whole summer. Weird, strange times, really nothing was as it seemed. I couldn't make any sense of what I heard or get anything that sounded truthful to me.

Telling others of the things didn't move anybody or get a reaction from them. They all thought I was just making up stories but I swear to you there was not one word of a lie passed my lips. Then one day a voice whispered in my ear, they spoke of a party that was taking place. I'd not heard of any such thing going on and knew my parents would not allow me to wander off to such a thing anyway. Still I had to wonder why this stranger was passing such information on to me.

Something must be done. Was I to act on this information or should I tell a person older than I? If only to be sure of my safety 'cos no matter what I had heard I had my doubts about these people.

Yet there was much needed to be done. A sudden fear seemed to have taken hold of me; I wanted to run! But from what? I couldn't understand. Suddenly a noise broke the silence that enveloped me. It was the party I'd heard of. Entering a room, one I'd not seen before, there were lifeless bodies with decaying skin. They were dancing to a music not heard any more. Upon waking with a dry throat, not to mention a throbbing headache, I reasoned it must have been a nightmare.

Andrew O'Reilly

Emma Purcell

Image: *Child*
Pencil on paper by Alice Purcell

Dad   1937–2005

What are you thinking now
as I sit here on the visitor's chair,
that you have lived your life and now it's your time to go,
or that it's just not fair, it's not your time?

What are you thinking now
as your morphine fuelled hands reach, carve, paint;
that your mother and father are waiting with outstretched arms,
or that you would much rather be here, as my father?

What are you thinking now
as the score from Inspector Morse draws our tears;
that all will be just fine, there will be no more pain,
or to hell with the suffering, you'll learn to live with it?

What are you thinking now
as the candle is lit and your rasping breath shallows;
that the weariness is overpowering, and you only want to sleep,
or is one more day too much to ask?

What are you thinking now
as the dust settles and our song is silent?

Extract from The Chinese Plum Tree

Prologue

Wed 24th November 1990

Age 8 years, four months and three days

I remember that she told me to wait there. Wait there on the swings. I thought it was a strange thing to ask a child. I don't think that I have ever just waited on a swing before. It suggests stillness and why be on a swing without motion?

 It was bright outside, but when I was woken from my slumber it had been dark. Too dark to be getting up and getting dressed. Too dark to be woken from my sweaty deep sleep. I dressed quickly in the dark, pulling on the clothes offered to me. She didn't seem to want to talk and I knew only too well not to interrupt the quiet moody atmosphere.

The car felt very cold inside, and my teeth started to shiver, but once we were on the move I started to warm up. She passed me back a Twix without apology. I didn't feel like chocolate. A bowl of Weetabix with warm milk would have been much nicer, but I took the bar and put it in the pocket of my red zippy coat. My scarf was wound tightly around my neck and my hat, the one that made my face itch, helped to keep the warmth in.

The car came to a sudden stop, and I must have been asleep as I was totally disorientated and had no clue as to what I was doing there. She told me to get out of the car. I used my sleeve to wipe condensation from my window making a space just big enough for me to see a playground with swings, slides and a climbing frame.

I shivered as I got out and tried to ignore the tangled feeling that had crept back inside me since I awoke for the second time. I wasn't sure what was expected of me. It felt peculiar. I felt peculiar. I looked at her but she wouldn't look at me. She kept her hands firmly in her pockets. That's when I noticed a pain in the bottom of my tummy. I thought it might be hunger so I took out the Twix and tore open the wrapper. At this point we were standing in front of the swings. I can still hear her voice telling me to wait there; that she forgot something from the car.

I watched from the swings as she drove away. I felt both fear and relief. I took a bite of the bar and sucked on it until the chocolate melted and the biscuit started to go soft. The playground was empty and I thought that if I stayed still long enough I wouldn't interrupt the quiet sound of leaves rustling on the trees. Just as I had entered my quiet space, a lady and a child came through the gate. I wondered if she was a mummy person or would she too leave her little boy on his own to play.

It seemed that she was very much a mummy person. Not only did she stay but she didn't take her eyes off him. Her gaze followed his every move; up the ladder, down the slide and she even took him on her knee to share a drink.

I looked on from my swing. How long would she be? What if it started to get dark and she hadn't come back for me? I didn't cry, instead I made a plan in my head. I would sleep under the climbing frame. I could shelter there and hide from scary things like dogs and foxes, maybe even wolves.

The mummy person walked towards me and I knew she was going to ask me something. I also knew that I was not going to be able to answer her as the biscuit part of the bar was fixed tightly to the roof of my mouth. She stopped and asked if I would like a push. I nodded. She made her way behind the swing and her firm hands on the small of my back felt reassuring. I longed for that touch with such anticipation every time I flew away from her, up towards the sky. I craved the feel of her strong hands on my back pushing me higher, higher.

A giddy gasp escaped from me. I couldn't control it. The sore feeling in my tummy turned to butterflies. Pretty free butterflies. I had started to slow down before I realised that the mummy person had stopped pushing me and was now pushing the little boy. He was beside me on the swing and was asking her to push him up high, as high as me. I felt very important and tried to use my legs to stay in the air.

He soon got bored, and before I knew it he was being zipped up and taken off home, out of the playground and out of my sight. Him and his mummy person. I remembered where I was and dragged my shoes along the dusty ground to bring myself to a stop. Looking around I realised that I was alone once again. I had become distracted by the loveliness of having someone look out for me, notice me. It started to rain and I thought of my hideout. It didn't look as inviting as it had before.

The Dispossessed

A short story

Six navy blue Louis Mulcahy goblets stand gleaming on the white wooden dresser. I have just put them there. It is the early hours of Sunday morning. Elizabeth washed them, and I dried and carefully placed them one by one in a circle and afterwards stood back to gauge the exactness of their perspective.

We joke again about the fact that we are the ones doing the dishes. Scrubbers! It seems hilarious through the haze of mulled wine fumes. The laughter is coming in waves from the living room above us. Sharp and shrill for two or three seconds and then nothing, except for the buzzing in our ears. Elizabeth stops mid scrubbing and cocks an ear to the floor above.

"Do you think they've all died or something?"

Our giddiness returns with revived enthusiasm.

Upstairs the New Year's Eve party is in full swing. We hear a toast being made. Crystal glasses clink in a fashion that would make the Penrose brothers turn in their graves. We float discreetly upstairs to join them. We mingle indiscernibly, catching snippets of conversation here and there, enough to put together some fine gossip that will keep us engaged for the rest of the evening. The living room has a bay window, the Christmas tree taking much of the natural light but giving much more back in glowing bursts of colour.

I am still for a moment, remembering something that I don't usually choose to remember but am jolted back by a sharp tugging on my arm. It is Elizabeth. She wants to go.

No. 57 Brighton Drive, Rathmines, Dublin 6 is the home of Pete and Julie Sweetman. The house boasts five stories from the converted basement where the couple spend most of their time, to an attic where many artefacts from tenants and owners past can be found in musty cardboard boxes. The basement has a kitchen, a living room and an office or music room, depending who is telling. The kitchen is painted white and cornflower blue and its like can be seen in any House and Home magazine. Julie had insisted on a Belfast sink ignoring suggestions about breakages.

Double doors divide the kitchen from the living room. The red leather corner suite takes up much of the space with a flat screen television in the corner. Wall to floor shelving holds their collection of books, cds and dvds. A Handful of Dust can be found on the second shelf third from the right, nine books from the left. It is sandwiched between Saturday and Never Let Me Go. No one seems to notice the fact that its pages are so worn even though Pete has only read it once.

The office holds an elegant double pedestal desk with a rich mahogany finish. Its drawers have antique brass plated handles. It had been a present from Pete's father. A painting of Julie as a child hangs on the wall. She is sitting by a patio window playing the harp. Her hair is long, fair and falling casually over her eyes. She has a wistful look as if she is lost in whatever music she is playing. The painting hangs strategically over the mantel. The actual harp stands in the middle of the room in front of a small stool. There is a patchwork cushion on the stool, made from old fragments of clothes that once belonged to Julie as a child. Her mother had made the cushion for her when she was eight years old. It now has many more patches and is somewhat thinner than before.

Julie and Pete sleep on the first floor. Their bedroom overlooks the small back garden where daffodils and tulips can be seen in abundance in springtime. Bursts of colour quilt the small patch. They gather like friends at a birthday party, in special bands of colours.

Julie and Pete moved to Brighton Drive three years ago on a cold January day. I remember it was two degrees outside and both the door to the basement and the front door were open for at least an hour and a half as the removal van was emptied. Elizabeth and I were keen to get to know our new housemates and we loitered in the hallways catching glimpses of personalities and preferences. By the time the doors were closed to the outside world we were chilled to the soul but quietly satisfied with the new arrivals.

Julie and Pete sold their house in Drumcondra deciding that they might in the future need more space. No miraculous additions to their family have arrived as yet and the rooms on the second floor lie empty apart from bags and boxes of unwanted bits and bobs that all households acquire. They compensate by throwing themselves wholeheartedly into every aspect of their lives, and that includes partying. They always throw a fantastic party for the New Year, the food carefully decided weeks in advance by Julie who has a particular flair for cooking. Creating food is an art, according to Julie. Her food creations appeal to all the senses. There is always a look of determination in her eyes as she works and Pete can be found watching her with a hint of sadness and empathy. Words don't come easy to Pete and I often find myself willing him to say something meaningful, or even just to say what is on his mind. It never works however, although sometimes I feel that I have influenced a train of thought. Elizabeth disagrees. She calls it coincidence!

We glide down the stairs to settle in for the night, tipping off the steps as we go. There are seventeen. I skip the last one having accepted that I'll never get there. The Sound of Music comes to mind. I am Liesel frozen in time. Elizabeth would have to skip three. I don't encourage her.

In the living room Elizabeth dances in a circle to a song in her head, closes her eyes and smiles. She used to play the piano. It was said that she had quite a talent and that makes me sad sometimes. When Julie plays the harp she sits and listens until the tears fall silently. She often cries herself to sleep. She tends to dwell on the past though. I try to teach her to be mindful but she usually falls at the first hurdle claiming some sort of distraction. Elizabeth always was the emotional one and a bit of a drama queen. I love her though and I feel a certain responsibility for her.

I go to the bookshelf and take down my nightly read. The repetition soothes me.

At twelve minutes past three I am awoken by noises of drunken goodbyes and taxi doors being shut with gusto. By twenty-three minutes past Julie and Pete come downstairs carrying the lazy man's load of glasses and leftovers. Pete turns on the light in the kitchen casting a glare into the living room. I allow my eyes adjust and throw a glance over at Elizabeth. She is still sleeping or at least pretending to be asleep for fear I might want to engage her in some mischief.

They leave the dishes on the countertop beside the sink. It irks me slightly. I was that rare child who never left the house without making his bed. My bedroom used to be my haven, a place where I could read, listen to music, dream.

Julie marvels at the tidy kitchen and is bemused at how their friends always seem to manage to do some sneaky washing up at parties. Her curiosity obviously short-lived, Julie switches off the light and follows Pete. I hear one set of footsteps on the stairs, they are heavy and laboured and I am sure they belong to him.

Then it comes over me, a gradual sensuous waterfall lightly tickling my outermost film. The opening fifths from Schindler's List are enough to capture me, enthrall me. I succumb. I am completely absorbed and relax back into my warm space.

The next thing I remember is Elizabeth flitting about, she has obviously been awake for a while. "Come on! We'll be late for God's sake!"

"What time is it?" I asked as I uncurl myself from my soul.

"It's five to and they're always there by around ten."

I went to where she was flitting and took her hand. "It's alright Elizabeth. It's alright."

Outside, the morning frost glistens in the early sunlight. It is going to be a beautiful day. Elizabeth turns to look up at the house.

"I love living here."

The front garden is paved with the sole exception of a willow tree whose bulging roots are causing cracks in the stonework. You can however avoid a bad fall if you take two small steps followed by one very long one, a trick I learned over the years. This, I learned the hard way after many a sore knee and broken pride. There is a black wrought iron gate about four feet tall and it whines in a glissando from an A above middle C to about a D. The tempo of the glissando depends on the force of the push. You can make a tune if you stand on the lower rung and swing slowly forward and back and then forward again until the gate can swing no further. It's no masterpiece but a very enjoyable way to while away the hours.

There is no time this morning to play games. We take off like two wayward kites on a blustery day and three minutes later we are there, looking over the sea of stone memories until our eyes see what they are searching for.

Two figures stand, side-by-side but not touching. They are wrapped up warmly against the January cold. They wear hats, one fur lined, the other a wool cap. Elizabeth and I do what we always do on this day. We make ourselves as big as we can and wrap ourselves around them. I close my eyes. I listen to their strong heartbeats and steady breaths. I put my head in the cradle of my mother's neck. I can feel her pulse. I then feel her smile. Elizabeth nestles into my father's chest.

After ten minutes or so they say their goodbyes, to us and to each other. As their cars drive off in opposite directions we fly off too, holding hands this time. We dance over the sleepy rooftops and float past our old school, closed for the holidays, the windows still clothed in festive decorations. We pass walkers, churchgoers, all night partyers and children on skateboards. When we reach the house we play hopscotch on the paving and compose a new tune on the gate.

"I love living here too," I say, and we go indoors.

The Spirit of the Dream Catcher

Visions of hope slip by
and I clasp strands of coloured light.
Scintillating they slip from my clutches
tantalise me, haunt me

They find your soul;
you linger,
sure of a creation,
a gift of beauty

Alas, once trapped,
they are no longer mine,
these glimpses of the past,
these crooked memories.

You give them sanctuary

Emma Purcell

Ag Súgradh le Chéile

... for Ann

What do you do when your friend tells you over the phone that her recently diagnosed ulcer is actually stomach cancer? After attempting to assuage her worst fears I pull the front door after me and walk the short stretch to my son's school. The daffodils in my front garden are huddled in bunches with their backs to the wind.

I face its northerly force welcoming the harsh aimless outbursts. My thoughts are numbed.

Two long minutes later I push the heavy double doors and find myself in a parallel universe. There in the school hall parents and their seven year olds stand in a circle while an energetic facilitator explains that we are going to sing a song together. I smile a lying smile at the other mums and I gratefully accept the bear hug from my son. The crook of his neck warms my cheeks. A tenderness attempts to dawn.

My thoughts, however, remain with my friend. As I put my right arm out and shake it all about I am thinking about the lonely, isolated place she is in at this moment. As I run around the hall trying to stick pegs on my fellow parents, and pull the felt tail from my son's pocket, I can't believe that two such different worlds can exist at exactly the same time. I see myself doing the motions although I feel that I am looking on through a grey mist of the unknown. I wonder how many other tragedies are hidden behind our masks.

Arriving back at work to teach a lively group of thirteen year olds, I try not to let them feel my mood. I, like most teachers, am a good actor.

Later that evening as I sit on the hospital bed my friend asks why. Why has it happened to her? My gut dissolves into moments from a Chopin Nocturne. The unanswerable question hangs there amidst the unfairness of life.

Leaving the faded foyer, I am momentarily blinded by the evening sun taking its opportunity to contradict. As I drive home I look up to try and find her window, and I wave just in case.

Emma Purcell

Stephanie Ripon

Image: *Beach at Lisadell*
Watercolour on paper by Stephanie Ripon

And To Stones

Cliffs, high, majestic, glistening in the rain, pelted jagged edges and crevices for white seagulls with their grey camouflage of feathers to nest. Flying, circling, fluttering and landing, a lonely cry echoing in those desolate places.

Below the cliffs, a sandy beach with beds of watered stones shining like gems in the evening light, hues of reds, oranges, pinks, purples and yellows, an orchestra of sound as they move with the pull of the tide.

These evening stones warm with sun under bare foot, comforting in their smoothness, a constant reminder of the aeons of time. Walking the shoreline, sand underfoot, occasionally a stone isolated with its water moat appears as an island.

Stephanie Ripon

Nature's Dance

The seagull soars
the seafarer gazes onto the empty horizon.

Trees circle a glade, rise to meet the blue
Yellow grasses sway, dandelion seeds float.

Insects buzz and hover, a bird warms her eggs
a green and yellow snake sidles across desert sands too hot to tread.

A stream trickles to the river, meets its estuary
spreads into freedom, is swept back to source.

Cascades of diamonds spill onto smooth rocks
make pools where coloured fish turn, swirl, dance.

Brightly yellowed scrub and gorse edge a rutted path,
a horned goat looks out from his desolate mountain.

Bonfires crackle, spit and sparkle,
smoke swirls into the arms of the wind, the bed of sky.

A woman sees the moon full, myriad stars,
knows of blackness without boundaries, black holes, far away planets.

The Traveller

This man was a traveller of detours, never quite being on his own road. The distraction of another path had always seemed greener and more enticing, more intriguing, somehow better than the ground on which he stood.

He was older now, withered, creased at the eyes from always looking ahead. There was loneliness about him, as if he had not shared himself for a long time, if ever. Unnoticed by him, the wind blew sideways at his coat, tugging at the unbuttoned edge. The rain fell softly, dampening his greying hair. He took a crumpled hat from his pocket and pulled it down over his head. As he did so a bird passed overhead, left droppings on his shoulder. He glanced at it sideways, noticed stirrings of annoyance in his mind. The coat was old and faded and had not seen a washing in many a year, and yet the pattern of the dropping annoyed him. He stood still for a moment and wondered at his annoyance. As the wind increased its strength he felt an urgency arise within himself that he could not understand. He stayed rooted to the spot at the crossroads. A stone toppled to the ground from a nearby wall with a thud. His ears felt the vibration through his feet; an awakening of sound, a sudden aftermath of silence. As he stood, he became aware of a space, a space in himself that felt strange, a space called 'stop'...

He felt forced to stay still, suddenly becoming aware of his breathing. Slowly at first he breathed, and then he began breathing more deeply. The breath travelled deep down his throat making a wave in his chest which rose as the enormity of his actions began to dawn. His nose twitched as he smelt the dampness of the air entering and leaving him. His hands tingled and his feet felt numb. Weary of travel on endless paths of seeking, he began in this moment at the crossroads to understand. An inner voice had knocked and screamed at him, but in a dark room where it could not be heard. Now a crack had opened in his heart and a voice began to sing. His voice. As he stood at the crossroads, he had been freed, by

> Wind dampened with soft rain,
>
> Grasses bent from willingness and acceptance,
>
> Shadows from clouds chasing across a sky,
>
> Saltiness of spray from nearby oceans.

TOM

He drifted off, his head giving a jerk as sleep wrapped him in a blanket of memories. The silence was broken occasionally by the crackling of sticks from the fire sparking and spluttering in the grate and the sound of his heavy breathing He drifted off, his head giving a jerk as sleep wrapped him in a blanket of from an old set of lungs. The room was in a half light, dust dancing, catching the evening sun from the west-facing window, a perfume of turf and cigarettes marking a fifty year span of time.

Pop's chair was tucked in beside the fireside, to the left and facing towards the window where he could watch for visitors and comings and goings. In the background his trusty transistor kept him up to date and sometimes crackled out tunes of long ago. His chair was a Windsor type fireside chair once bright with patterns in velvet reds and creams, now worn and more the colours of wines and greys, its cushions taking his shape over many years of use. He could stretch out his long legs in front of him without causing obstruction.

As he breathed heavily, he remained in a half sleep with his memories. As clear as the very first day he could see Mary's sweet rosy face. The first dance on their wedding day. It was like yesterday, or so he thought. Time had stolen his youth and had also stolen Mary. The children had come and gone, babies crying, gurgling, toddlers laughing, playing, fighting, schools, lessons, teenage tears and pranks and then off to find work in finer bigger places, with phone calls once a week.

His suit, the grey one, still fitted him. How strange, he thought. Was it Sunday? He dozed again, head nodding, the warm comfort of his eyelids soothed him as distant sounds disappeared.

The loud click of the door latch jumped him from his reverie. "Hello, Tom!" a loud, efficient voice boomed into his consciousness. That wretched woman, he thought. Come to tidy, fuss and cook, bringing him back to reality. How he wished to sleep the big sleep and once again join his Mary on the dance floor.

Nora Ryan

Image: *Killavoggy N.S. Co. Leitrim, 1952*

Decorating the Beetle

"The Devil finds work for idle hands" still resonates as clearly in my mind today as the day my father shouted that at me, when he caught me giving his dear Volkswagen Beetle what in my mind was a well-deserved face lift. I had very carefully chosen the brightest and most decorative wallpaper I could find from discarded rolls lying abandoned in the shed. "This will be a great surprise for my Dad" I thought as I got busy with the work in hand; paper, paste and brush all lined up ready to go. I was a very artistic seven year-old, everybody said so. As the papering progressed I would stand back to admire my handiwork. "Dad will be very proud of his young daughter" I thought to myself. I imagined him driving in style to the nearest village in his unique car, secure in the knowledge that he would get nothing but admiring, and perhaps a few envious glances, from those he was sure to meet on the five mile journey.

Task almost complete, I stood back in awe. Gosh I really was a genius! All I had to do now was stick down a few loose corners that evaded the paste and a good job was satisfactorily done. At precisely that moment a thunderous roar from the upstairs bedroom window almost shattered my eardrums. My father had half his body hanging out the window with a look of disbelief on his face. "What in the name of God do you think you're playing at? Are you completely mad? What have you done to my beautiful car?" he screamed, choking with rage. "Don't move from that spot until I get down to you". That wasn't exactly the reaction I had expected. bottom lip started to quiver. I waited with fingers crossed in the vain hope that when Dad took a closer look and saw the lovely job I had done he'd be delighted. The kitchen door opened with a crash and there stood both parents.

I wasn't sure what my safest course of action was, should I make a run for it or stand my ground? What was wrong with them, couldn't they see how beautiful the car looked, hadn't they any taste at all? I couldn't bear the silence any longer and ventured in a very timid voice "Doesn't it look beautiful Daddy?" My mother burst out laughing which only added to my father's rage. He made a lunge at me "You little brat" he roared " you know the Devil finds work for idle hands, do not come back into the house until you've removed every speck of paper from that car while I think up a suitable punishment for you".

That was where my wallpapering career began and ended!

First Steps

My first encounter, or first consciousness of the 'Supreme Being' who inherited the earth, was when I was told as a child by my grandmother to polish my brothers' shoes for Mass on Sunday. I refused point blank to do this and said that the boys were big enough and ugly enough to clean their own shoes. My grandmother was outraged at my disobedience and informed me, in a very stern voice, that neither my father nor any of my uncles had ever polished their own shoes. Their sisters always did it as part of their womanly duties. I smartly replied 'Signs on them'. No sooner had I uttered these words than my grannie smacked me very hard on the back of my bare legs. 'You'll soon learn your place Missy' she said 'Looking after men is woman's work and never forget'. I decided at this stage not to risk another slap, so I walked away defiantly from her singing "Gotta wash that man right out of my hair".

The following Monday I skipped off happily to school. There was a great buzz of excitement in the classroom. It was the day the priest was coming for the Religious Examination. As the school clock chimed the hour, the priest arrived. Like John Wayne on his white stallion, he called one of the boys out to take care of his horse while he made a grand entrance, whip in hand, hoping to, and in most cases succeeding, in putting the fear of God into our hearts.

We lined up around the classroom as he shot question after question at us. If any one of us hesitated, he cracked his whip off the desk or floor making us more terrified than we already were.

God help the poor unfortunate who failed to answer correctly or who hesitated before answering, they found themselves at the receiving end of a lash of the whip. He picked on the girls all of the time and told us how stupid we were and how much smarter and more intelligent the boys were.

By now I was so mad that I put up my hand, and though the priest kept ignoring me I kept shaking it until he had no choice but to notice me. 'Well young miss, what do you have to say for yourself?' he boomed.

I was shaking like a leaf but the annoyance I felt at his utter contempt for women overcame my fear. I asked him in a very calm, clear voice, 'Father, if women are as thick and stupid as you say how come God chose a woman to be the mother of His Son instead of a man?'

The slap he gave me across the jaw with the back of his hand sent me reeling across the floor and caused a palpable shock along the line of pupils. I didn't react which maddened him even further. The satisfaction of having annoyed him made up for the ringing in my sore head. The clackity clack of the heels of his boots on the floor as he shot out of the classroom door, whip still in hand, was music to my ear.

However, having to face the Master, my father, who was mortally embarrassed by his daughter's altercation with the priest, is a story best left for another day… !

Ladies over 33 – Earn an Extra €500–€1,000 before Christmas – genuine company...

Ladies over 33 – whatever can this mean?
Are we wanted for our bodies
Or just to cook and clean?
I doubt it's just to walk the dog
Or bring turf in from the bog...

This money is a tempting offer
T'will add great value to the coffer
I'll answer this before I'm late
They won't know I'm past my "Sell by" date

The Trimmings

Seeing symbols of religion or good luck charms calls to mind a gyrating Elvis Presley singing 'Come on and be my little good luck charm uh-huh-huh…'

When Rural Electrification was still a long way off, we very often did our homework by candlelight. Back then in every home, there hung somewhere on the wall a picture of the Sacred Heart, usually lit up by a small red-globed oil lamp. When lessons were done we were made go down on our knees to say the Rosary. The Rosary itself was a doddle, it was the "trimmings" that nearly killed us –

We prayed for
Those who asked our prayers,
Those who needed our prayers,
Those we promised to pray for,
Those with nobody to pray for them,
For the most abandoned soul in Purgatory,
The most abandoned priest's soul in Purgatory,
The farmer down the road whose cow is sick,
The ulcer on poor Biddy's leg,
The next door neighbour's sheep savaged by a pack
of stray dogs…

By this stage, my mind was far away, visualising Elvis in his white suit, hips swinging to the beat of the music and gazing at me beneath smouldering lashes. My father, seeing the rapturous look on my face, nudged my mother, nodded towards me and whispered," Ah here we have the making of a fine nun, thank God".

The Ballroom of Dreams

Where have all the years gone? I don't remember them passing. I close my eyes and let my mind drift like a lazy river flowing along gently, in no rush. I remember driving past the Ballroom of Romance in Glenfarne one day, remember the urge to see if I could get a peek inside. I parked my car and went up to the door…

… Millions of butterflies play havoc with my stomach. How many times have I walked through this very door in high spirits, full of anticipation of what the night might hold? Would I meet the man of my dreams tonight and be swept off my feet? I see the sign with the entry fee: "Ladies 1/6d, Gents 2/6d (or 'half a crown').

I push the door and much to my surprise it opens with a slight wheeze. I roam around for a while trying to recapture the atmosphere. Memories flood my mind and overwhelm me. The feelings I experience take me by surprise and leave me shaken. Unbidden tears for my lost youth fill my eyes. I hadn't expected to feel so emotional. I sit down on a rickety old armchair propped up in the corner, try to regain some control, dry the flow of tears tumbling down my cheeks. What would I do if anyone were to find me here blubbering?

As I sit I look around the old familiar place. The crystal ball still hangs from the ceiling, unmoving now. There is no cascade of multi-coloured lights bouncing off the walls, the floor, the band and the dancers. The ceiling and the crystal ball are dull, festooned with varying cobweb patterns. Up above me is the balcony where one could have tea, coffee or soft drinks – no Vodka or Red Bull. If you were lucky and the guy you fancied on the night asked to buy you a mineral or a cup of tea you knew you had "pulled" as the saying goes. I dream on, hear Brendan Bowyer singing his lively Hucklebuck, I see myself and all my friends dancing to the beat as we "twisted all around". Dickie Rock slows the pace down while we go with him "From the Candy Store on the Corner to the Chapel on the Hill". If the fellow you had your eye on asked you to dance as this song was announced you were on your way in your imagination to that very same chapel on the hill! Now it's Larry Cunningham's turn to take us in a lovely romantic waltz to "Lovely Leitrim, where the Shannon waters flow". I'm getting tired now, dancing and dreaming.

My shoulder is being shaken and reluctantly I open my eyes. I must have dozed off. I look around to get my bearings and remember where I am. "Missus, Missus, are you O.K? I'm the caretaker, can I help you?" My eyes open fully. No Brendan, Dickie or Larry. No shining crystal ball. Just dust on the windows and dirt on the floor – like the words of the Eagles when they sang "Seems like a dream now, it was so long ago…"

Jean Tuomey

Image: *Reverie*
Ink on paper by James Tuomey

A Moment

The low December sun
shines through chalky clouds;
reflects on the new lake

Had the field not been flooded,
the sun not so low,
the clouds not so milky,

the moment would be otherwise.

Jean Tuomey

Impermanence in Tuscany

Sometimes I'm back there
on a chair slotted in the narrow door frame
overlooking the olive grove.
Spiegel im Spiegel plays in their gallery.

He washes the coffee cups,
she goes to the waterfall to bathe,
and I, not home, am home,
listening to Pärt's music.

The sky can be blue,
wine can come from down the lane,
a ruined cottage can be restored,
and cream can curdle.

In the Hospital

I need to walk into the garden,
water lettuce heads now fully grown,
see orange in marigolds squeezed
between beetroot and onions.

I need to hear the thrush sing,
watch Sam, tail high,
charge the stone wall,
vain effort at warding off intruders.

I need to check the beans,
tie up the loose ones, walk anywhere,
see everything, do anything
other than witness you grow frail.

Jean Tuomey

Our First Hour

The hospital silent,
patients asleep,
trolleys not yet wheeling.

We stared at his stillness.
Someone made us tea,
others repositioned him.

Then his song wafted
down the corridor
as if from another world.

The Rose of Tralee
leaked in under his closed door.
For the first time he did not join in.

Sky Food

Golden light slices
into the horizon as the train moves west.
The colours reduce;
orange dulls to yellow,
then glazed magnolia, jasmine on the side.

For dessert the sun serves its full face,
flambéed stripes
of pink and purple
pointing into burnt orange.
By nightfall, I am replete.

Jean Tuomey

The Bell Tolls

Sometimes I don't think and then you are here,
or in the garden,
face to the sun, tea cup in hand,
paper folded beside you.

I notice I can drive
past the hospital
without indicating,
without flinching.

I notice we are all busy,
keep moving,
keep talking,
traffic at a roundabout.

As the bells in Sligo ring,
I see you carry me to the font.
In October they carried you too –
your last time.

The Notebook

Christy opened his front door and looked across to the field opposite his garden. He had slept well last night. He was on call. It was the lambing season and he had expected a disturbed night. He had grown accustomed to interrupted sleep over the years. Since a holiday in Venice ten years ago he had built short siestas into his day. Maria had taught him the benefit of his post lunch nap. Just twenty minutes was sufficient. He still remembered the lunch they had in St Mark's square, when just by chance they shared a table and four hours later they were still drinking coffee.

Christy turned from the front door, tidying the mat in the porch. He returned to the kitchen. Better not to think about Maria, better to check his diary, see if he had any calls to make before he opened his practice at 10am. "Today, the first day of Spring I am going to make some changes" he resolved. He sat at the kitchen table, already set for one and swallowing his porridge steeped since last night he flicked through The Weekly. No order at all in its layout, he noticed.

Looking around the kitchen, its cleanliness satisfied him. Only a large pot on the draining board. He had celebrated his forty seventh birthday the previous night, cooked his favourite meal, bacon and cabbage, and now while drinking a mug of tea, opened the hardback notebook Ann had sent him. "This may help you sort your social life!" she had written on the inside cover. He regretted admitting to his sister that his life was out of balance. She had phoned the previous Saturday morning and when he had replied negatively to her question about his weekend plans, she had said "Christy, forget Maria, that was ten years ago. You knew her for a few days. Time you organised your life." So he decided he would make a list of fictitious plans if she ever opened the topic again. Might even throw in a female name just to really take the pressure off. Once again Fiona had forgotten his birthday. He, of course always remembered hers, and the children's and Mike's too.

The notebook was long, about nine inches, and four inches wide. He would write down ten things to do this week. Of course he would not tell Jim about the notebook. They could continue to discuss golf, football and reflect on their teenage years of fishing but personal stuff, that was out of bounds. Though planning to keep the notebook on the left-hand side of the second drawer in the kitchen and never to take it out of the house, he wrote his address on the inside flap. The Lane, Carrowbuine, Shannon Park East. He smiled, there was no Shannon Park West or South or North but he was particular and this was to be a notebook of truth so the address had to be accurate.

He glanced at the kitchen clock. 8.45. Hurry up, he muttered. He often talked to himself. Broke the silence. "Just get the first page full and then its over to Keogh's". He planned to check them first on his morning rounds. They were a young couple, new to farming and their lambs were starting to arrive. He loved to see the excitement on their faces.

Holding the pen tightly he glanced at the newspaper and saw a list of evening classes starting the following week. Improvers Italian. No, not that. He was moving on. Next on the list was scuba diving. So he wrote

1   Scuba Diving Sat 10am

That should please Ann. Underneath he wrote 2 and glancing out the window his neglected garden caught his eye.

2   Thurs 7. 30–9. 30pm Grow your own vegetables. Byrne's Garden Centre.

He had seen the notice in the corner shop last night. All welcome, it had said.

3   Sun 2-4pm golf.

Yes, time to ring Joe and suggest a game. They hadn't played since last October. Whistling now, Christy closed the notebook, opened the second drawer and tucked it under the folded tea towels. He would complete the list before his siesta today. Then he would ring Ann and suggest they meet for a drink after work on Friday to mark his birthday. Though he would thank her for the notebook, his list was not on his conversation agenda.

Biographies

Café Writers – A First Collection

Peggie Gallagher lives in Sligo. Her work has appeared in literary journals in Ireland, England and North America. Peggie has been shortlisted for the Strokestown International and the Gregory O'Donoghue poetry awards. She was the Winner of the prestigious Listowel Poetry Collection prize in Spring of 2012, and her first collection, *Tilth*, was subsequently published by Arlen House in winter, 2012.

Maura Gilligan is a writer and community arts facilitator. Born in India, Maura has lived close to Knocknarea Mountain and the Atlantic for most of her life. Her poetry has won prizes and has been broadcast and published. She has co-created plays, performance pieces, short film, and imagery for the national Bealtaine Festival for many years.

Liam Maloney is a Sligo-based scribe. Maloney has been writing valiantly since the mid-1990s and first found inspiration via a collection of Grimms' fairy tales that arrived in a parcel his mother brought from America. A Pepsi drinker on occasion, when he isn't writing he likes to look at cloud formations, listen to a wide spectrum of music and jog slowly.

Ann McKirdy was born in Sligo and raised in Belmullet. There she developed a love for the rugged beauty of Erris and the wild Atlantic shoreline of the West of Ireland. It was there too that she became aware of the power of language. Ann lived overseas for a number of years and upon returning joined a writing workshop facilitated by Maura Gilligan which rekindled her passion for language and the written word.

Síle Ní Chuirc is a Gemini, which means she moves from one subject to another in the same sentence, and that is quite confusing for the people in her company. Being a lover of beauty and Nature, she would call herself a Pantheist, like her favourite artist, Frida Kahlo. Her favourite Author is Patrick O'Brian, favourite movie, Dr Zhivago, and if sent to live on a desert island would bring her lipstick.

Eamon Ó Cléirigh, originally from Dublin, is living in Sligo since 2003. Writing is his passion, both long-form fiction and poetry, and he spends as much time as he can within its loving arms. He hopes one day to get his novels out there for all to see. For now, he's enjoying what is a lifelong learning process.

Biographies

Andrew O'Reilly came to Sligo from his Dublin home base in 2006 to do a one year course in the IT. He fell in love with Sligo and is still here. The first things to enthrall him were music, films and books, but during his time at the IT he was introduced to creative writing and it has been a part of his life ever since.

Emma Purcell is originally from Co. Dublin but is now living in Sligo with her husband and two children. She is currently teaching music in Grange PPS. Emma joined a creative writing group in September 2009 facilitated by Maura Gilligan and it was here that her love of writing was nourished and encouraged. Emma's short story *The Dispossessed* was one of four winners of The Lonely Voice competition in the Irish Writers Centre in April 2012. An extract from her Novel *The Chinese Plum Tree* was shortlisted for the Author rights Agency competition on Arena in September 2011. She joined the Café Writers in December, 2011, and looks forward each week to the chats, the cakes, and of course the writing..

Stephanie Ripon became a member of the Café Writers' group in its initiation and has found writing, just like painting and working in ceramics, a great way to express herself. For Stephanie it is about the feelings and emotions that arise from the written word and how descriptive text can bring the reader into a visual space. Her aim is to combine her writing with her art work.

Nora Ryan, a native of Leitrim, has been living in Sligo for over forty years. A retired primary school teacher, Nora enjoys drama, her favourite role playing cat-loving Rita in Bernard Farrell's 'I do not like thee Dr. Fell'. She has been with Cafe Writers since its inception. She previously attended creative writing classes in St. Michael's Family Life Centre with Maura Gilligan, Peggy Gallagher and Ann Devaney.

Jean Tuomey was born in Sligo, grew up in Dundalk and currently lives in Castlebar. A teacher for 23 years, she now facilitates writing groups in Mayo and trained as a writing facilitator with the National Association for Poetry Therapy in the States. Her hobbies are walking, being in nature, growing vegetables and writing. Reading modern fiction and poetry are a staple part of her diet.

Table of Illustrations

1   *To a Child Dancing in the Wind*
    Maura Gilligan

2   *Hands*
    Liam Maloney

3   *The View from our Kitchen*
    Sarra McKirdy

4   *Istanbul Street*
    Síle Ní Chuirc

5   *Lough Gill*
    Eamon O'Cleirigh

6   *Cafe Arabica, Sligo*
    Andrew O'Reilly

7   *Child*
    Alice Purcell

8   *Beach at Lisadell*
    Stephanie Ripon

9   *Killavoggy N.S. Co. Leitrim, 1952*

10 *Reverie*
    James Tuomey